Emergency Preparedness for Apartment Communities

THE WORKBOOK

A Neighborhood Disaster Survival Guide

Virginia S. Nicols

Dentrovisi, Inc.

Irvine, California

Copyright © 2019 by **Virginia S. Nicols**

All rights reserved. No part of this publication may be reproduced, distributed or transmitted in any form or by any means, without prior written permission.

Dentrovisi, Inc.
4790 Irvine Blvd., Suite 105
Irvine, CA 92620

Book Layout © 2017 BookDesignTemplates.com

Emergency Preparedness for Homeowner Communities – THE WORK-BOOK - Virginia S. Nicols -- 1st ed.

ISBN: 978-1-6914456-5-3

A Message to Residents

Why are we publishing a workbook to accompany our *Emergency Preparedness for Apartment Communities*? We put a lot into those original 125 pages. Why would we want to add still more?

The answer is simple.

Emergency Preparedness is a big topic. And apartment communities, while varying widely in their physical construction and community status, present specific opportunities for – and challenges to – becoming organized for emergency preparedness. A single book on the subject is simply not enough to effectively provoke people to action. Hopefully, this workbook will serve to help jump start that process.

Even when you read a book, and even if you can remember everything you read, **that doesn't necessarily translate into your actually DOING anything!**

So that's what this workbook is for.

It's meant to help you sort through all the information and focus on just what you need to get your household prepared. Then, step-by-step, copies of the workbook can help more members of your community get prepared.

In our opinion, preparedness is not an individual family thing. We believe . . .

When disaster hits a community, we are all in it together!

Of course, we can't guarantee survival. By definition, disasters are unpredictable and can be deadly. But when disaster hits a *prepared* community, we believe . . .

- More people will be **ready to respond and confident** in their response even in a chaotic situation. And the more people that are prepared, the safer everyone will be.
- More **"first responders" will step up** in the immediate aftermath, while we wait for *official* First Responders to show up – maybe hours or days later.
- **People needing extra help** will be more likely to be identified and cared for.

The book lays all this out. Now, with the workbook, we hope to move more readers to action.

What's the best way to use the workbook?

We've set up the workbook as a series of questions that roughly follow the chapters in the book. We assume you have a copy of the book, so from time to time we'll make reference to specific detail there. We've given you plenty of room to write answers, comments and "to-do" lists.

You probably want to start at the beginning of the workbook and make your way through to the end. Skip over questions that don't fit your family or that you've already dealt with. On questions where you're not sure about your first answers, let the workbook serve as a brainstorming tool. Mark it up with comments, arrows and exclamation points!

(We are big believers in the value of physically writing things down. We think writing helps memory and understanding in a way typing on a tablet or computer just can't match.)

In the end, the amount of effort you a put into the workbook will determine its true usefulness.

Now, we may re-write it a few times in the future as we learn about new ideas. By following us on the website https://EmergencyPlanGuide.org you should get any updates you need.

Virginia Nicols

P.S. Thanks in advance for comments at our site and reviews of our books on Amazon. Your personal involvement can help us improve our materials and reach more people.

PREFACE

Like a lot of people, I was motivated by the events of 9/11 to do something for my community. When the city where I lived offered CERT training (whatever that was!), it sounded like a good idea.

Community Emergency Response Team training was much more and much better than I expected. But it became clear that . . .

> *. . . after the training I had valuable knowledge but no good way to share what I had learned.*

So, my partner Joe Krueger and I started building a more robust emergency organization in our immediate neighborhood. (There had been a rudimentary group even before CERT came into being.)

Soon we took on leadership positions. We set up a more formal structure and operating procedures. And we've helped keep the group active ever since.

Our neighborhood group has a number of CERT grads in it, but is made up mostly of "untrained" folks who simply care about their neighbors. So while many of our activities are based on national preparedness concepts, we try to make things **simpler and easier than what the government has to offer!**

The book *Emergency Preparedness for Apartment Communities* and this companion *Workbook* (and, in fact, all our published volumes in the series!) follow the same principles:

- Basic info in one convenient package
- Step-by-step processes to be completed at your own pace

- More resources for those who want them.

I hope this book will be enough to get you started or, even better, keep you going! I look forward to hearing how you have been able to use the information with YOUR neighborhood group, too!

A final note: Just as the range of styles, type of construction and size vary widely among apartment buildings, many neighborhood areas include both single family homes as well as apartments. Your neighborhood may require reference to our book, *Emergency Preparedness for Homeowner Communities* and its companion WORKBOOK as well as the Apartment version. Be prepared to improvise as necessary for your particular area and situation.

Virginia Nicols
Emergency Plan Guide

If you haven't yet signed up to receive our Advisories, please do so now. We come out with new material — and sometimes important old material — usually every week. You can sign up on any page of our site: https://EmergencyPlanGuide.org

Contents

INTRODUCTION

Before we start outlining the positive actions you can (and should) be taking, it's probably a good idea to address some obvious factors that make this version of our workbook series different. First, as a resident of a "multi-family housing structure" (pardon the technical reference to your home), you will have a very different set of challenges in accumulating and storing emergency supplies. Second, your relationship with your neighbors will be markedly different than were you living in a single family dwelling (sfd).

Unfortunately there are simply too many different types of apartment, condominium and multi-family structures for us to address each specifically. So I have kept my specific recommendations mostly to personal actions you can take, leaving you to adapt those to your specific living situation. If you follow our regular discussions and blog entries at EmergencyPlanGuide there will likely be a number of specific Advisories that address individual situations similar to yours.

Let's begin where YOU are starting, and get an idea of your own priorities. There will be a lot more to come on each of these subjects, of course. And you'll be faced with quite a few choices, far more than we can anticipate . . . so, be prepared to improvise!

But for now, five easy questions:

Introduction -1: Have you ever experienced a real disaster, whether natural or man-made? What was it, and when?

Introduction – 2: What was your first reaction? How did your feelings about the disaster change as time went on?

Introduction – 3: Have you experienced a *recent* emergency in your current home, apartment or residential community? What was it? How did you respond?

Introduction – 4: How did your neighbors respond to the emergency?

Introduction – 5: What role did these past disasters play in forming **your current attitude** about being prepared? What other things that are going on today are impacting your attitude about being prepared?

OK, with this perspective, let's get on to the real action! We think the following three things are the most important things you can do to ensure survival, so **start with them in mind**:

1. Make it a habit to keep your vehicles' fuel at least ½ to ¾ full.
2. Know where all members of your household are at all times, and how you plan to communicate and reunite if separated.
3. Have survival kits with snacks, water and medicine for 1-3 days in every vehicle – and rotate contents regularly.

PART ONE – YOUR PERSONAL SAFETY

The "list" of what emergency supplies you should have or would *want* in case of an emergency can be endless. Recently, I saw an article entitled "The 10 most important items for your stash of emergency supplies" followed the very next day by "The 100 items you absolutely need to store in case of emergency!"

After 17 years we have come up with a simplified list to get you started:

Eight categories *of emergency supplies essential*
for personal safety and security.

And you need enough of each of these:

To carry you through without electricity or
outside assistance for at least three days.

The way things have been going, 3 days really isn't long enough. We think it makes more sense to aim for a 10-day or 2 week supply. Start small and grow your stash slowly and steadily. Everything you do makes you better off than you were yesterday!

If you haven't already made these preparations, why not?

- ☐ Too much to remember.
- ☐ Can't afford them all.
- ☐ Don't have any room for them in my home.
- ☐ Spouse doesn't believe in emergency preparedness.
- ☐ Just can't seem to get around to it.
- ☐ My excuse: _______________________

OK, we'll see what we can do to overcome these, as we go. The fact that you have invested in this book is a VERY good sign that you are, in fact, ready to get around to it!

WATER

Wouldn't you think water to be the easiest of all to have ready? In fact, it's consistently one of the most difficult, particularly for people living in houses on small lots, apartments and mobile homes! As you go through this workbook, you'll see why.

We start from the very beginning.

Water – 1: How much water do you need for yourself and your household, including pets? The minimum: 1 gallon per person per day times 3 days. For a 4 person household, that would be 1 x 4 x 3 = 12 gallons. Do the arithmetic for your household:

The answer above is the MINIMUM. You really should be storing water for longer. **Multiply your answer by 10** to get a more realistic number of gallons you should be considering!

Water – 2: Do you have a pet? How much more water should you store for your pet for 10 days?

Water – 3: Certain households might need more water than the 1 gallon minimum. Does your household include small children? Pregnant or breast-feeding mothers? People with medical conditions? How much more water should you be storing for these people?

Water – 4: What's your grand total of gallons for an extended emergency? Add the numbers you got from Questions 1, 2 and 3. (It's a BIG number – and that's why water is always at the top of our "difficult" list!)

Water – 5: Where will you store all this water?

Gallons and gallons of water take up space and weigh a LOT. Both space and weight need to be considered by residents. In addition, in some buildings, you need to be particularly careful about avoiding leaks, because floor coverings and drywall can get soaked from leaks, deform and even disintegrate, causing major damage below.

Consider a combination of storage containers like these described below. *Hint*: In our community, **we have more than once been able to make GROUP PUR-CHASES** of water and water barrel containers that made it cheaper for everyone. But, many apartment communities, especially high rise, have no space for barrels.

55 gallon barrel – is still the very best if you have room for it and/or partner with neighbor/s. Yes, you have to condition the water every year (add bleach or disinfect-ant) but one or two barrels may be able to conveniently meet all your emergency water storage needs. **A 55-gallon barrel belongs outside** (out of the direct sun-light) or in your parking space or in a shed. In either place, raise it off the ground with a wooden frame. Be sure you get a pump and bung wrench and store them nearby. And remember, a full barrel will be too heavy to move, so pick your spot carefully.

How much will a new 55-gal barrel cost? (Typically between $50 and $100.) Where could you put barrels of water?

Stackable water "bricks" — Rigid, stackable plastic containers like those shown below come in a variety of sizes and are great for safely storing emergency water. They are not cheap, but their flexibility and durability can't be beat. The most popular bricks are about the size of a large shoe box, so they can be fit and stacked into a number of empty spaces: on the floor of a closet, in the well of a desk, under the bed. Wherever possible, stack full containers against outside bearing walls. (At about 30 pounds each when full of water, you can also carry them relatively easily.)

How many water bricks can you find storage for?

Plastic water containers in freezer — You can kill two birds with one stone (efficiency and emergency supplies) by filling up all the extra space in your freezer with plastic containers of frozen water. Refresh regularly; if the water doesn't smell fresh, use it for watering plants, washing your feet, etc. (Square or rectangular shapes are more efficient than round. Leave room for the water to expand as it freezes.)

How many containers do you already have that you can use? (Don't use containers that have held chemicals, gasoline, etc.)

Commercially packaged water – You can buy aluminum can six-packs of water (50-year life!), plasticized soft packs or even paper cartons that can be stored just about anywhere you have space -- maybe behind books on your book shelves? (Check the shelf life of packages when you buy.) If you have no room for larger containers, these may work!

Fill-at-the-last-minute containers – If you learn in advance of an approaching storm or power outage, consider filling rigid or expandable containers for temporary emergency water storage. There are a variety of them to consider: buckets (also foldable models), plastic water bags and bladders, even bathtub liners for one-time emergency use!

What large containers do you already have that could be used to hold emergency water for a few days?

Bottled water from the store – If you have the room, you can certainly consider storing extra bottled water purchased in liters, quarts or half-gallons. Our favorites are the square, strong plastic Fiji water bottles, because regular round bottles do not pack efficiently and do not stack. (Even a plastic-wrapped case will eventually collapse and start leaking . . .!) If you do choose bottled water, it will likely be good for at least 6 months. (Check the date.) And avoid the "environmentally friendly" thin plastic bottles for storage. The thin material decomposes. They also may **deform and collapse within weeks!**

How much of your emergency water needs will come from commercial bottled water?

Water – 6: Do you plan to store any **home-filled containers**? You certainly don't want to run the risk of drinking contaminated water, so become an expert on safety practices for storing water over the long term, whether it comes from the tap or a local well. Treating water, or "conditioning" it, is sensible and not expensive or difficult. (At Emergency Plan Guide we cover water storage in detail.)

What disinfectant or conditioner will you use to protect home-filled water containers?

Water – 7: Finding and filtering water once you've run out of your stored supply is a separate topic. Your location and the type of disaster will have a lot to do with the condition of water you can come up with. This is a topic for discussion with neighbors – see Part 2 of this workbook! In the meanwhile, try to store as much clean water as you can, so you will at least have a few days to work out a longer term solution if necessary. And, in case you think swimming pool water is good for drinking, think again. If you've kept up on your house cleaning and maintenance, water from your toilet tanks and hot water heater can also help meet your immediate needs for the first day or so.

FOOD

Now that we have water dealt with, things get a lot easier!

In a real emergency, assume the power will be out. Food in your refrigerator and freezer **will start defrosting on the very first day!** Moreover, with no power, you may not even be able to cook any of it before it spoils.

So, we have to think about food that doesn't need refrigeration or cooking. At the same time, we have to think about food VALUE. No, chips don't take refrigeration and they don't require cooking – but you can't live for days on chips alone!

Food – 1: What canned or ready-to-eat foods do you have in your cupboards right now? List everything! (Hopefully, you have some peanut butter and a few cans of sardines, tuna and chicken.)

Food – 2: We assume you like the items on the list above. Take another run-through and CIRCLE the items that would fall into the category of "healthy." (high in protein; rich in vitamins; contain fiber; etc.) (If you have kids, get them to help you with this!)

Food – 3: Our best advice? Lay in a larger supply of the "best" foods from your regular shopping list – that is, those foods that are circled. Simply buy a few more every week and add them at the back of your regular shelves. Eat from the front, and replace at the back. Easy!

Food – 4: Now, take another look at your list. What's missing? If you usually cook with fresh ingredients, ask yourself how you can replace them with canned equivalents. Canned tuna and canned chicken are favorites and have the same nutritional value (or more) than fresh. Same with vegetables (beans, tomatoes, corn) and fruits (apricots, peaches). Look for self-opening cans, and avoid high sodium if possible.

What canned foods should you add to your list for emergency eating?

Food – 5: Don't forget some added flavor! Yes, you can eat beans out of a can with a spoon day after day, but that will get real tiring mighty quick. Be sure to have a supply of condiments to perk things up – mustard, catsup, soy sauce, hot sauce, etc. Condiments won't spoil! Pick up extra packets at your favorite fast food restaurants.

What packs of condiments should you add to your emergency supplies?

Food – 6: But wait! I have a camp stove and can heat water!

I'm sure you've noticed there has been no mention of dried foods (rice, beans) and the staples we all have in our kitchens, like flour, sugar, etc. No mention of instant coffee or hot chocolate! Unless you can cook, you won't get far with these – and that includes most "survival meals" – that are freeze-dried or powdered and that take **lots of water and heat** to reconstitute.

Do you have a camp stove or BBQ that you know how to operate? How much fuel do you have and how long will it last? (And do you have a fire starter?) Note that these

STOVES MUST BE USED OUTSIDE, NOT IN THE HOUSE to avoid carbon monoxide poisoning. Does your apartment have an outside patio or balcony?

Food – 7: Along with food, consider your need for a manual can opener, utensils, dishes, and a way to clean up after your meals without hot water. What "extras" should you add to your list? (Regular campers will have an advantage here.)

MEDICINES, PRESCRIPTIONS AND FIRST AID

In a big emergency, you may not be able to get to a pharmacy and even if you can, their electricity may be out, just like gas stations, super markets and ATMS. Even if their door is open, they won't have lights, won't be able to check records or accept payments – and may be a target for looting.

Try to keep at least a week's worth of prescriptions on hand at all times so you don't have to even attempt to get to the pharmacy immediately.

(We understand the challenge of convincing your doctor to prescribe a whole week's worth of prescription pills to store for emergencies. Put on as much pressure as you can. We always apply for a refill a couple of days before we run out, and thus come up with a couple of extra pills each month! As with everything else, keep refreshing your supply of prescriptions.)

IF YOU HAVE PRESCRIPTIONS THAT NEED REFRIGERATION, you must consider how you will protect them in a power outage! Some recommendations:

- Find out the safe temperature range for your medicines. (Some may not really need refrigeration.)
- Be ready with an insulated cooler that you can promptly fill with ice to protect medicines for at least a few days.
- In an emergency, could a different formula of your medicine work, one that didn't need refrigeration? Check with your doctor.
- Consider purchasing **a solar-powered refrigerator/freezer** and know how to use it in an emergency. (Costs start at around $500; most seem to be more like $1,000.)
- A small generator is sufficient to run periodically to support your refrigerator. However, you'll have to consider its weight, noise, and how and where to store fuel for the generator. Again, do you have an outside balcony where emissions won't pollute (poison) living areas?

Medicines – 1: Do you have an emergency supply of all the prescriptions you are taking?

Medicines – 2: What plans do you have for safeguarding medicines/prescriptions that need refrigeration?

Medicines – 3: Old and outdated first aid creams, Band-Aids, ointments, etc. can be worse than useless. Do you need items now that you didn't years ago? How about items appropriate for a real disaster, like BIG gauze pads, stronger disinfectants, sunscreen and sunglasses, bug spray, mask, a tourniquet, etc.?

What's the state of your first aid kits? Make a list of items you need to add to your kit/s.

EMERGENCY COMMUNICATIONS

When the electricity goes out, so does T.V., phone service, and cable internet. You may have a cellphone connection but only if towers haven't been damaged – and your batteries are still charged.

If you are calling for help, or simply to notify family members that you are safe – you have to know what number/s to call!

Communications – 1: What emergency contact numbers do you need to **write down** and have handy, or better yet, to **memorize?** (This is particularly important for children.) Do you have numbers for out-of-area contacts (in other states) who can help you communicate with family members when local lines are overloaded?

Communications – 2: Do you have a landline in your home? (You know, one of those "old fashioned" phones that plugs into the wall.) It may function when nothing else does.

Communications – 3: Do you have rechargeable portable phones in your home – with a base that is plugged in? They will NOT function in a power outage!

Communications – 4: Do you have a cell phone with **a way to recharge it without having to plug it into the wall**? Options could include: a portable battery charger ("power bank") (2-3 charges) or a solar charger (takes time but works).

Communications – 5: Do you know how to text on your smart phone? In an emergency, when the system is overwhelmed, a voice call may be blocked but a text message may get through! If you don't text, is there a child nearby to teach you ☺?

Communications – 6: If your TV and internet are out, you'll want to get the news via a battery- or solar-operated emergency AM/FM/NOAA (weather information) radio. Some of these connect to computers, tablets and smart phones, too. Do you have at least one emergency radio in your supplies? (At our website we tell you what to look for in the way of emergency radios. It's our most popular page! https://emergencyplanguide.org/reviews/emergency-radio-reviews/)

Communications – 7: If you have planned in advance, you may find that you can communicate with nearby family members and neighbors using battery-operated walkie-talkies. Do you have walkie-talkies? Does your neighborhood, management or homeowners association have an emergency response team that uses walkie-talkies? (They are inexpensive and actually have lots of non-emergency, recreational uses.) We actually keep a walkie-talkie in every room in case someone is trapped.

EMERGENCY LIGHTING

In a major disaster, total darkness is likely to be one of the big surprises. With no light coming in the window from streetlights, and no lights inside the home, we'll probably have no choice but to stay put until daylight comes.

Even limited light will make a big difference in our comfort and safety! So, what are our options?

Lighting – 1: Handheld flashlights are a must. Just one flashlight won't do if you have to struggle through a damaged apartment to find it! How many flashlights do you have now and where do you keep them?

Lighting – 2: What sort of back-up battery power do you have? In a power outage, rechargeable batteries may be quickly used up! Options: supply of extra alkaline batteries (in multiple sizes), or a solar charger.

Lighting – 3: A flashlight is fine for directing light, but not very useful if you need to move around, prepare meals, make repairs, etc. (We've all held a flashlight in our mouths when needing to use two hands for a job!) Do you have battery-operated lanterns or headlamps as emergency lighting sources?

Lighting – 4: You may have other light sources, such as solar-powered pathway lights, battery-operated night lights, glow sticks, candles, etc. **Note: candles represent major fire hazards and are NOT advised if there is any chance of catching curtains or the possibility of a gas line break!** What other lighting sources do you have?

STAYING WARM AND DRY

Your apartment may be undamaged, but your heating system may still be off in an emergency. Staying warm will be essential to your well-being – and is likely to require a purchase or two.

Warm and dry – 1: Dry bedding is the first and easiest item to be sure you have on hand. Do you have quilts or sleeping bags stored where they will stay dry?

Warm and dry – 2: What warm clothing and boots can you count on if you had to spend time outdoors? Do you have any rain gear, even a simple poncho? (This may be a particularly important question for older people who normally avoid going out in bad weather or at night!) Heavy duty trash bags can be cut to form makeshift ponchos to keep dry and provide some warmth.

Warm and dry – 3: What emergency sources of heat are available to you? There may not be many options. Do you have a fireplace and extra fuel? Is it safe to use? A camp stove could heat up water for hot chocolate, but is NOT appropriate for room heating. A proper-sized generator, positioned outside the home, might be able to run an appropriately-sized room heater – but will NOT run the furnace. Which of these options do you want to do more research on?

LIMITING AND/OR REPAIRING DAMAGE

Different events change the kinds of physical preparations you may want to make to your apartment. For example, in earthquake country it simply makes sense to fasten furniture to the wall (particularly TVs and bookcases) and to move heavy items to lower shelves instead of storing them up high. In hurricane zones, you may want to board up windows and position sand bags. Moreover, older homes may require one type of preparation or repair, while newer homes require something different.

Duplex, triplex and quads present one tyope of challenge. Two, three and four story apartment buildings offer quite another. High rise apartment buildings resemble office buildings in many respects. We cannot cover all the options here in the WORKBOOK; one of the best resources on preparing for different events can be found at https://Ready.gov.

If your home has been damaged by an event, you may need to perform immediate repairs to improve its ability to shelter you from the elements. Here's where a supply of tools make sense. Check the tools you know how to use. Circle supplies you need to buy and store. But, keep in mind that, even in emergency situations, you may be limited in what you are allowed to do in the way of repairs or, for that matter, mitigation.

☐ Lighting   ☐ Hammer, nails and wood

<table>
<tr><td>☐ Duct tape</td><td>☐ Saw, knife, scissors</td></tr>
<tr><td>☐ Plastic sheeting</td><td>☐ Pry bar</td></tr>
<tr><td>☐ Strong light weight tarp</td><td>☐ Pliers, screw driver</td></tr>
<tr><td>☐ Rope</td><td>☐ Other</td></tr>
</table>

Note: If you own your apartment or condo, your insurance may cover damage from a storm. Take photos to prove your loss before you start on any significant repairs. If you do NOT own the home, changes or repairs to the home may not be welcome. You will have to weigh them against what you feel is necessary to protect your family.

For consideration: Tools can be expensive, and have to be stored. Good neighbors may be able to share both the cost and the space.

SANITATION

This is likely to be one of your biggest challenges, and critical for health. If the entire neighborhood has been hit by the emergency, you can assume that it will only take a couple of hours before your toilet may no longer flush and will begin to back up.

Be prepared with **heavy-duty plastic trash compactor bags**! These are bags that fit right into a toilet bowl, or over the rim of a 5-gallon bucket. Use the bags to collect waste, then close the bags securely and store in a designated place outside.

Sanitation – 1: Do you have trash compactor bags on hand? You will likely need more than one bag per day.

Sanitation – 2: Do you have a camping potty or a 5-gallon bucket (preferably with a lid) you could use as a temporary toilet?

Sanitation – 3: How will you keep yourself and the area clean? Put these items on your shopping list if you don't have them already:

- ☐ Toilet paper (enough for 10 days for the whole household)
- ☐ Rubber gloves and paper towels
- ☐ Moist wipes
- ☐ Pine Sol, Clorox or other disinfectant (pour some into the bag before sealing it)

PERSONAL PLAN

Pulling together and storing supplies at home assumes you will all be there to use them. And that may not end up being the case! Your household also needs to make plans for how to respond if something happens and members are spread out.

Personal Plan – 1: Can everyone get out of the apartment in an emergency? Do a walkthrough and even draw a map that identifies **two exits** from each room if possible! (Do windows open? Can you actually get through and down to the ground?) In multi-level structures – and especially high-rise buildings – elevators may not work in emergencies. Can you use an escape ladder? What are your options?

Personal Plan – 2: Where will you meet if your home is damaged or uninhabitable?

Personal Plan – 3: Do you have contact names and numbers, and in particular an **out-of-town contact name and number**, so you can let people know you are OK?

Do you have that number MEMORIZED? (I know, we already covered this once. It's worth covering twice!)

Personal Plan – 4: Have you discussed evacuation and what that might be like, particularly with children, elderly, handicapped or pets? (It may not be possible to make assumptions about evacuation routes before an event, but a discussion will alert family and household members of the need to be ready.) Does management have a plan for evacuation of the building? Has the apartment owner even addressed emergency preparedness? What are their responsibilities according to local and state regulations? List things you want to research.

PROGRESS REPORT

SHELTER-IN-PLACE. How are you doing so far in being prepared to shelter-in-place after a disaster? If you've been able to answer most of these questions positively, you are WAY ahead of the average American! In fact, just going through the questions and considering the answers will have given you a much better awareness of your situation – and that alone is a big part of preparedness.

SURVIVAL KIT FOR EVACUATION. When it comes to evacuating, planning focuses on your survival kit – or kits. Each member of your household – and each pet – needs a survival kit to last for at least 72 hours! Pets need carriers or cages.

Your kit will likely have items from the same eight categories we've discussed already, but of course it has to be compact enough to be carried (duffle bag? backpack?) Most importantly, it has to be **packed and ready BEFORE the disaster hits**.

Survival kit – 1: How many kits do you need for your household?

In addition to water, food, prescriptions, a flashlight and batteries, emergency radio, phone and charger, jacket and rain poncho, heavy duty trash bags, compactor bags, extra underwear, duct tape and multi-tool, your survival kit may also need:

- ☐ Personal care items, different for each person (toothbrush, tampons, extra glasses, etc.)
- ☐ Personal comfort item: teddy bear, book, bible, etc.
- ☐ Copies of important documents (best if scanned onto a flash drive) and account information – banking, home ownership, insurance coverage, etc.
- ☐ Emergency contact information
- ☐ Some cash (lots of quarters, small-denomination bills, $1, $5, $10 & $20.)
- ☐ And perhaps: whistle, gloves, face mask, protective glasses or goggles

PET SURVIVAL KIT. Your pet's basic kit should include:

- ☐ Pet carrier
- ☐ Leashes
- ☐ Pet ID (photo of you with pet) including vaccination documents
- ☐ Pet food and dishes
- ☐ Pet's medicines and first aid items

You must assume that your pet will NOT likely be allowed into a disaster shelter, so search out in advance places where your pet might be able to stay if you have to leave home.

PART TWO – COUNTING ON YOUR NEIGHBORS

So far, we've examined in some detail what every individual household can do to prepare for an unexpected emergency. Being prepared is ***your*** responsibility – no one else cares as much as you do, or even has the duty to protect you. (You might want to review our comments about "The Authorities" and your "Property Managers" in Part One of our book, *Emergency Preparedness for Apartment Communities*.)

In most communities, however, you may not be entirely on your own! You likely have neighbors on all sides. How do you think they will respond?

- Do you even know your closest neighbors?
- Will they be able to help you, or will they turn to you for help?
- Or will they turn ON you for help?

Part One of the Workbook dealt with people's responsibility for having basic supplies to carry them through an interruption or upset. Hopefully your neighbors have done so.

Now in Part Two, we're going to take a broader look at "the neighborhood."

In the immediate aftermath of a disaster, you won't be thinking about supplies. You will be concerned with surviving for the next few minutes! And the people first to step up to help will be those very neighbors we've mentioned.

In a disaster, the real "first responders" are the
people next to you.

Happily, statistics show over and over again that neighbors ARE willing to step up and help. The better they know you, and the more skills you and they have, the more people will survive.

Part Two focuses on building a stronger community response based on neighbors' relationships and skills.

GET TO KNOW YOUR NEIGHBORS

What do you know about your immediate neighbors? Consider a survey of a few neighbors like this one:

How prepared are your neighbors?

Answers to these questions about a *sample of your neighbors* will help your group decide on the best steps for the whole community.

1. Are they likely to be home (during the day, at night)?
2. How physically able are they?
3. How mentally or emotionally capable are they?
4. How are their communications skills?
5. Do they have any training that would be helpful in an emergency? (CERT, medical, military, construction, law enforcement, counseling, etc.)
6. Do they have tools or equipment that might be useful in an emergency?
7. Do they have a car and do they drive?
8. Would they need extra help in an emergency?
9. Do they have pets or children that need to be considered?
10. Have they done anything to set aside emergency supplies?

Obviously, these questions can't be answered unless you know people personally!

Neighbors – 1: In our estimation, the very first step toward getting your community or neighborhood organized is for **a few active residents to answer questions about their immediate neighbors**. Who do you already know who might be willing to help find out more about their own neighbors (based on questions like those above)?

Neighbors – 2: Share the questions and give people a chance to get answers. Then schedule an informal get-together to compare notes.

- How many in your original small group actually collected info about their neighbors?

- How many capable and/or interested residents were they able to identify?

Neighbors – 3: If you have identified **a half-dozen or so capable people**, you have the start of a real emergency preparedness team effort. (Fewer than that and it will be an uphill and discouraging battle.) If your preliminary survey suggests you have **as many as 20% of the community interested**, you will be able to make a VERY BIG difference! ! What's your estimate?

GET MORE TRAINING

We have found that for neighbors to work easily and effectively together they need to have the same goals and guiding principles. This is where CERT (Community Emergency Response Team) training comes in. When people have taken the course, they have some big advantages they can bring to bear for their community:

- Standardized vocabulary
- Shared experiences
- Basic emergency supplies and tools
- A track to run on

And perhaps most important, they enjoy a degree of respect from neighbors that reflects their knowledge and training . . . respect they can't get any other way.

Training – 1: What CERT training is available in your area? Where, when, cost? (If you have a big enough group, you may be able to attract a trainer just for your team.)

Training – 2: If you can't get into a class, what is available online? (Check here: https://www.ready.gov/community-emergency-response-team)

INTRODUCE THE TEAM CONCEPT

With a core group of CERT-trained neighbors, your organizing can really begin. You'll have confidence and credibility! Here are steps to consider as background research.

Team – 1: Meet with your Apartment Management and/or local HOA to understand their responsibilities and duties with regards to preparedness and to learn about any plans they may have made. What has already been done in your area to prepare for emergencies? (Staff training, evacuation routes, list of local resources, etc.)

Team – 2: Plan a kick-off meeting for the neighborhood. You need to meet face-to-face for people to understand the importance and urgency of preparing. Use the following items to decide with your core group what makes sense for your community. **Get core group members to volunteer** to take on different jobs, and/or to find other neighbors to help them! (People always seem to wait to be invited . . .!)

- ☐ Where to hold the meeting
- ☐ Best time for meeting
- ☐ Neighbor or guest speaker?
- ☐ Educational handouts (from local government, speaker, city agencies)
- ☐ Advance publicity (flyer, poster, website, email announcement, telephone announcement)
- ☐ M/C and welcome committee – nametags, sign-in, map of community, etc.
- ☐ Audio visual equipment – screen, projector, microphone
- ☐ "Call to action" or next step (Sign up for CERT training? Volunteer to be on a research committee? Distribute info about emergency supplies to other residents?)

And remember, a door prize and refreshments are always popular!

(We have put on hundreds of emergency group meetings. Every group is different and you may find some useful suggestions in: *Emergency Preparedness Meeting Ideas*. It also has suggestions for room layouts, comments about group safety, activities, etc.)

ENGAGE YOUR COMMUNITY

Your kick-off meeting will give you a good idea of what the next step should be. We have found that it takes time for people to embrace new ideas! After your kick-off meeting, **plan agendas for several monthly or quarterly meetings.** The book, *Emergency Preparedness for Apartment Communities* has a number of ideas for appropriate topics – which of these might work for you?

- ☐ "Show and tell" featuring neighbors' Survival Kits ("Here's what I put my stuff in, and here's what I have in my kit.") (See Appendix in *Emergency Preparedness for Apartment Communities*.)
- ☐ Guest speaker from Fire Department or Police Department on "What you need to know about evacuation."
- ☐ Brainstorm or small group activity on "What threats should we *realistically* prepare for?" (Long list in Appendix of *Emergency Preparedness for Apartment Communities*.)
- ☐ Demonstration of using the improvised potty bags usually draws real laughter. ☺

☐   What emergency supplies should we have, and what preparations should we make for shelter-in-place, given the most likely emergencies? (Arrangement with local contractor? Local hardware store?)

☐   Upcoming CERT classes! (Always on our list!)

Try to involve more and different people as you put on each meeting. People who come to the meetings will be the people who become part of an emergency response group. What would be some good topics for your group, and who could help put together each of these meetings?

PART THREE -- BUILDING YOUR NEIGHBORHOOD PLAN

If you have enjoyed a successful kick-off meeting, and your core group is still intact and enthusiastic, you are well on your way to being able to build a more formal preparedness plan for your neighborhood. Why do you want a plan?

In a big emergency, you and your neighbors are the real first responders. How effective your response will be depends on the plan you've made and the training you've done. There is no time for planning or for training once the emergency hits.

Because every community is different, and each neighborhood group has different skills, different levels of commitment and different resources, we can't promise a straight-forward process for putting a plan together. And once you have built your plan, we know it won't be useful for very long without regular updates!

What follows are ideas that we have used, with varying degrees of success, to build and maintain our group. I recommend that you pick the ones that make the most sense for you – and get started! Everything you do, perfect or not, will help your community to be better prepared.

"NEVER DOUBT THAT A SMALL GROUP . . . CAN CHANGE THE WORLD."

The full quote from Margaret Mead: "Never doubt that a small group of *thoughtful, committed citizens* can change the world!" Research done by your small group can lay a strong foundation for the community!

Small Group – 1: Does a plan already exist? We've previously mentioned checking with the HOA. Check with long-time residents, too. Build on what's been done.

Small Group – 2: Who plays a key role in your neighborhood? It may take a while to identify all the different suppliers and stakeholders, but connecting with them is essential. Put together a master list of names and phone numbers. Start with:

- ☐ HOA Officers as well as owners and managers of rental property
- ☐ Utilities (gas, electricity, water, sewer)
- ☐ Maintenance and repair staff or contractors
- ☐ Landscaping
- ☐ Security
- ☐ Police and Fire department
- ☐ Insurance
- ☐ Other __________

You may encounter some reluctance from people who aren't used to dealing with residents. Tell them what you are trying to accomplish. Invite them to participate as experts. These people will be important resources.

Small Group – 3: Identify the threats faced by the area. Brainstorm "What could possibly go wrong?!" It will be easy to start with natural and weather-related events (storms, earthquakes, hurricanes, tornados, etc.), but be sure to expand your thinking **to include accidents or emergencies in the broader community**. (You may want to have a city map handy for this brainstorming session.) For example, consider threats posed by:

- ☐ Rivers and lakes
- ☐ Railroad tracks
- ☐ Water treatment plants
- ☐ Nearby airports
- ☐ Military installations
- ☐ Manufacturing or other production facilities

    ☐ Retail centers

    ☐ Schools

    ☐ Etc.

The Appendix of the book, *Emergency Preparedness for Apartment Communities,* has a list of over 70 possible threats!

Small Group – 4: Select the top 4 or 5 types of disasters you want to focus on and prepare for. Choose the most likely, not necessarily the most dramatic. (Most likely? A power outage!) Who can start assembling educational material on each of these?

Small Group – 5: Which of your top disasters will require evacuation? Are any evacuation procedures already in place? Check with community groups, American Red Cross, property management companies, police and fire department.

Small Group – 6: Find out about utility shut-offs. Broken gas lines and fire are major hazards in many areas. Your community may be served by the local utility and/or a private utility company. Generally residents won't have occasion to take steps to shut off common or apartment-wide utilities, but they might if managers or utility workers aren't available. (Be aware that information about utilities may be difficult to obtain even for fire authorities. Natural gas is supplied by high pressure lines to communities, reducing pressure by time it reaches individual households. Shutting off one large service area can result in sudden and dangerous pressure increases in other areas disturbing the overall balance of pressure) Would a map of the area, showing gas lines and shut-offs, be useful? Your leadership team may want to keep this information confidential.

NEIGHBORHOOD GROUP ACTIVITIES

Your small group has done enough research now to be able to give a larger group of people the confidence that emergency preparedness not only makes sense, but is do-able.

What follows are a number of steps that build on your small group research. I've tried to put them in some order, but you can pick and choose, divide and combine, however it makes sense for people in your area.

As a reminder, our recommendations about organizing teams are based on FEMA and CERT guidelines. We recommend you follow their lead so that as you interact with professional emergency responders, the vocabulary and concepts will be familiar to you and helpful to them.

> *And one more reminder: YOU ARE ALL VOLUNTEERS! You don't have to follow any neighbor's "orders," and they don't have to follow yours. The only way community organizing works is if everyone works off of the same playbook, is treated with respect – and earns it.*

Neighborhood Group – 1: What exactly makes up your apartment community, your "neighborhood?" Develop a map that shows:

- ☐ Building floorplans (your floor plus above & below) . . . your apt. neighbors
- ☐ Property boundaries (and neighboring properties)
- ☐ Adjacent roadways, entrances and exits (official and emergency)
- ☐ Roads, bridges, gates, etc.
- ☐ Streets and parking areas
- ☐ Street lights, fire hydrants
- ☐ Community clubhouse/office/maintenance areas
- ☐ Etc.

Convert your map to digital format (Take a photo, scan.) so you can share it. We use our map all the time with new neighbors, new volunteer group members, new fire fighters and police, etc.

Neighborhood Group – 2: What threats does your neighborhood face? Consider conducting another brainstorming session to **get more people involved** in thinking about what might happen. (They may bring different experiences and memories to the discussion – considerations that were missing the first time around.) List (again) the top 4-5 threats you will focus on.

____

____

____

____

____

Neighborhood Group – 3: What assets are you starting with as you prepare for the top 4-5 threats? First, share your written list of resources (from Part Two) to get the conversation started. Then, consider how to find out more about resources within and adjacent to the neighborhood. (Here's an Inventory Worksheet from Emergency

Plan Guide. https://emergencyplanguide.org/inventory-worksheet-for-a-resilient-community/.) What skills & equipment do you have that will most likely be needed?

Neighborhood Group – 4: Based on your map and what you know so far about your neighbors, what's the best way to divide your community into zones and teams? For apartment buildings, depending on size & number of apartments, a Division (40-75 apts.) might be an entire building or just one or two floors. Be creative and flexible taking length of residency, ages, family structures, ethnicity (language factors) into consideration.

Neighborhood Group – 5: Build your preliminary organization chart. On the next page is a simple diagram of what the picture might look like. Your Incident Commander manages the incident, working through a communications team. Divisions are the logical area zones.

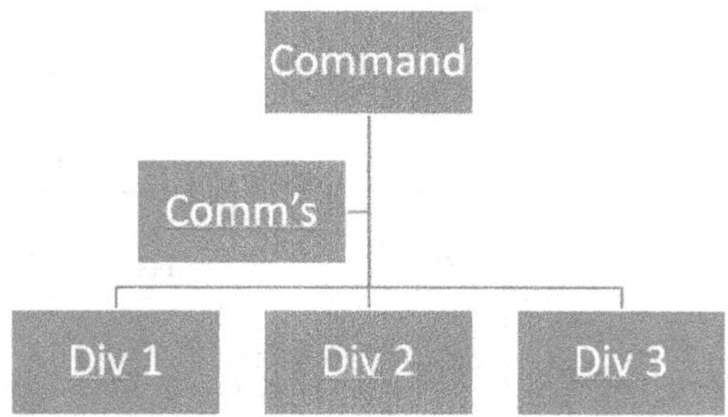

Each division has several block captains who are assigned to cover a group of several apartments, as shown below:

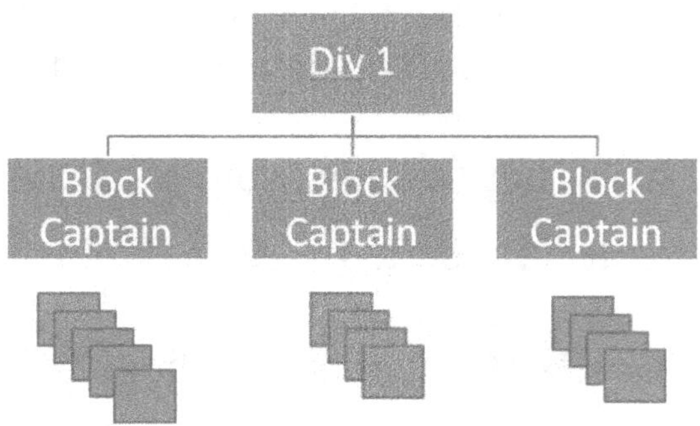

These charts are a **very simplified version** of FEMA's Incident Command System (ICS). Learn more about ICS here: https:// EmergencyPlanguide.org/NIMS). What does your preliminary chart look like? Draw it with empty boxes first!

Neighborhood Group – 6: Staff up! We are fast reaching the end of the easy part. Now comes a longer period of time in which you and neighbors reach out to find other interested volunteers to fill positions in your Neighborhood Emergency Response Group. Here are some of the positions you'll be looking to fill:

Block Captain: A Block Captain has a simple but essential job. Having enough Block Captains will always be a challenge! Here is a potential block captain job description:

- Be ready to confirm your own safety first.
- Check on apartments on either side to be sure your home isn't threatened.
- Check on your assigned neighbors' and their well-being. Write everything down.
- Report in to your Division leader so help can be sent as appropriate. (We use walkie-talkies for reporting, assuming other communications will be out. More on that later.)

Division Leader: Knows his or her Division, communicates with Block Captains in emergency, then transmits their info to the Incident Commander.

Communications ("Net Control") manages radio communications from and to the Incident Commander to Division Leaders. In a small group, Communications may be handled by the Incident Commander.

Incident Commander is "the first qualified person to arrive at headquarters." All CERT members are prepared to take on the role of Incident Commander, and cede command when someone more qualified shows up. The Commander, with the assistance of Division Leaders and other Special Teams, tracks community conditions and dispatches Special Teams when possible. The Incident Commander turns over control of the incident to official First Responders when they arrive.

Special Teams may or may not be available to you. We have been fortunate in the past to have qualified residents interested in heading up teams such as:

- Search and Rescue
- Triage and First Aid

- ☐ Damage Assessment and Control
- ☐ Care and Shelter
- ☐ Security
- ☐ Logistics and Power

Real Life: Setting up and staffing this many teams is a lot of work and may not even be required or possible in your community. No matter how hard we try, we never have people in every position. Try to have additional volunteers as backup. (You can count on the fact that some members of your team will not be available due to work, vacations, illness, etc.) We list all the teams here, though, because these are the teams suggested by CERT. Just considering them gives you a better grasp on what your community might face in an emergency.

Neighborhood Group – 7: What supplies can you provide for your participating group members? How will you manage the purchase, inventorying, etc.

- ☐ Copy of written plan (see next section)
- ☐ Walkie-talkies (multiple channels can be assigned to divisions & teams)
- ☐ Maps that show buildings, homes, service areas and major terrain features
- ☐ Reflective vests
- ☐ Clipboards, pens
- ☐ Etc.

Neighborhood Group – 8: How will members communicate in an emergency? (Assume electricity is out and cell towers are down.)

SUMMARY WORKSHEET FOR THE GROUP BUILDING PROCESS

Neighborhood Organization Process Based on CERT

Step One

One or More CERT Graduates Emerge as Leaders

(Someone steps forward. At least two more CERT Graduates are needed.)

Step Two

Formation of Leadership Group 3 to 5 CERT Graduates

(Now, with 3 - 5 CERT Graduates The Leadership Team is in place.)

Step Three

Leadership Group Launches an Emergency Preparedness Publicity Campaign

(Flyers advertise CERT classes and include preparedness checklists.)

Step Four

Build List of Responsive Residents in the Neighborhood and Identify Their Specific Interests

(Teams of 2 CERT Grads call on neighbors, promote preparedness & CERT.)

Step Five

Setup a Series of Neighborhood Meetings with Authority Guest Speakers

(Schedule and Hold Weekly Meetings of the Expanded Leadership Group.)

Step Six

Divide Neighborhood into Sectors or "Divisions" and Assign Two or Three CERT Members

(Continue house calls by teams of two CERT Grads.)

Step Seven

Expand Group Interest within Each Division, Recruit Additional Volunteers for CERT and Identify More Leaders

(Begin Holding Monthly Meetings & Building a group Preparedness Plan.)

WRITING THE PLAN

Ultimately, you'll want to draft a written plan that describes your group's set-up and its mission. Only a written plan will:

- Give you credibility with your HOA, property owners, insurance company, etc.
- Reassure local police and fire authorities as well as neighbors, and particularly new neighbors, that you know what you're doing
- Serve as the basis for keeping the emergency program going, as some neighbors leave and others move in

If you have reached this point in your organizing, you probably already have a good idea of what you want in your plan. Keep it simple and easy to read.

Written Plan #1: Which of the following sections might you want in your plan?

- ☐ Introduction – Why you are writing a plan, and how it came to be
- ☐ Overview of your community -- description of size, layout, geography, etc.
- ☐ Threats facing your area based on your brain-storming sessions
- ☐ Make-up of your volunteer Emergency Response Team (for example, Incident Commander, Division leaders, Block Captains, Special teams)
- ☐ Description of roles of each member of the team as well as property managers
- ☐ List of resources available to the community including map showing residences, utility shutoffs, fire hydrants, etc.
- ☐ Communications protocols – How will people be notified of emergencies? How will Emergency Response Team members communicate among themselves?
- ☐ Process for standing down when official responders arrive

Written Plan #2: Who will actually write the plan? There is no need for one person to take on the whole job. Different members of your group can draft different sections, and one person can assemble and edit. (In our experience the written plan is regularly being updated.) Do you have volunteers?

Written Plan #3: How many copies do you need? The Master Plan is what gets up-dated; volunteer members may find a summary plan perfectly adequate.

PRACTICING THE PLAN

Practice #1: What is your goal for practicing the various aspects of your plan? Communications, preparation for various threats, etc.?

We find that different groups set meeting schedules to meet their needs – sometimes they hold monthly meetings, sometimes quarterly, sometimes only when there's a particular concern. (Start of fire season. Start of hurricane season.) We have consist-ently mixed different training programs with monthly walkie-talkie practice and updates from our local first responder community. You'll want to mix up your meetings, too. If you want suggestions for meetings, our companion book *Emergency Preparedness Meeting Ideas* has notes from over 17 years of our experience!

Congratulations. You've reached the end of this workbook. But this is actually just the beginning of building a real emergency preparedness program in your community. It's actually a process that never really ends, so try and find ways to make it fun and interesting to be a volunteer.

For now, take a look back to see what you and your group have accomplished. Even if you haven't done everything outlined in the workbook yet, every action you have taken is a step toward greater security and peace of mind. And remember that we are on your team. Stay in touch with us by regularly checking in at our website where we share recommendations, experiences between communities as well as newly published official data. https://EmergencyPlanGuide.org

More About the Author

Virginia S. Nicols and her partner Joseph Krueger, with various CERT, FEMA and American Red Cross trainings to their credit, head up their neighborhood emergency response group in Southern California. Throughout their 25+ year career in direct marketing, they have designed emergency planning programs for a wide range of businesses.

What started in their local community as a purely volunteer effort has developed into something bigger. Because of their marketing and organizing skills, Joe and Virginia were called upon – and wanted – to provide more and more educational materials, equipment recommendations, etc. Their website EmergencyPlan-Guide.org was the result. Its Advisories keep Joe and Virginia busy (as if they weren't busy enough!) and help support their volunteer efforts.

The website and their volunteer work have also inspired 7 volumes in the *Neighborhood Disaster Survival Guide* series. This workbook now adds a 8th volume! Find out more at https://EmergencyPlanGuide.org/Neighborhood-Disaster-Survival-Guide-series/

Questions or comments? Don't hesitate to contact Virginia at:
Virginia@EmergencyPlanGuide.org